I BELIEVE

I BELIEVE

Allan Stark

**STARK
BOOKS**
an Andrews McMeel
Publishing Imprint

00 01 02 03 04 TWP 10 9 8 7 6 5 4 3 2 1

ISBN 0-7407-0574-1

Book design by Holly Camerlinck

INTRODUCTION

◆ ◆ ◆

It is one thing to think about or have an opinion about family, friends, people, teams, manners, music, movies, Elvis, religion, restaurants, Tina Turner, naps, et cetera, and quite another to form personal views about those subjects.

Thoughts are continuous and are as automatic and natural as the heartbeat. Beliefs, on the other hand, require self-examination, analysis, and commitment. Beliefs just don't happen. They are formed and shaped by each person.

The *I Believe* journal is designed to help you think about your beliefs, but it certainly can't help you determine what those beliefs should be. Writing down your beliefs is an interesting, challenging, fun, and important process. As American novelist William Faulkner said, "I have found that the greatest help in meeting any problem with decency and self-respect and whatever courage is demanded, is to know where you yourself stand. That is, to have in words what you believe and are acting from."

One of my favorite movie scenes illustrates what Faulkner said. It comes from the baseball movie *Bull Durham* when veteran minor-league catcher Crash Davis (Kevin Costner) says the following to baseball groupie and eventual girlfriend Annie Savoy (Susan Sarandon):

> *Well, I believe in the soul . . . the small of a woman's back, the hangin' curveball, high fiber, good Scotch, that the novels of Susan Sontag are self-indulgent, overrated crap. I believe Lee Harvey Oswald acted alone, I believe there ought to be a con- stitutional amendment outlawing AstroTurf . . . I believe in the sweet spot, soft-core pornography, opening your presents Christmas morning rather than Christmas Eve, and I believe in long, slow, deep, wet kisses that last three days.*

What impressed me wasn't what Crash Davis believed, but that he knew what he believed. Thoughts make us human, but beliefs give us individuality.

I've written down more than seven hundred of my own beliefs and collected them in my book, *I Believe*. I've included one of them at the bottom of each page in this journal. Think of them as idea starters. Think, examine, review, reflect, read, and listen, and then start writing down *your* beliefs. It is a journey well worth taking.

Allan Stark

I BELIEVE

FAMILY

_____

_____

_____

_____

_____

_____

_____

_____

_____

_____

_____

_____

_____

_____

_____

_____

_____

_____

◆ ◆ ◆

I believe it when my children say to me, "I love you."

FAMILY

_____

_____

_____

_____

_____

_____

_____

_____

_____

_____

_____

_____

_____

_____

_____

_____

❖ ❖ ❖

_I believe my mother is in heaven and that she will
always let me know what she thinks of my decisions._

FAMILY

◆ ◆ ◆

I believe my brother is totally trustworthy.

FRIENDS

◆ ◆ ◆

*I believe it's okay to talk about religion
and politics with your friends.*

COUPLES

❖ ❖ ❖

*I believe husbands and wives should do
everything possible to protect each other when life
becomes difficult or cruel.*

LOVE

◆ ◆ ◆

I believe in love at first sight.

ACTORS/MOVIES

❖ ❖ ❖

I believe **The Lion King** *is the best Disney animated movie ever.*

SINGERS

_____

_____

_____

_____

_____

_____

_____

_____

_____

_____

_____

_____

_____

_____

_____

_____

_____

◆ ◆ ◆

I believe Bob Dylan brought in the 1960s.

EDUCATION/TEACHERS

◆ ◆ ◆

*I believe parents should get to know their
children's teachers.*

MY COUNTRY

◆ ◆ ◆

*I believe in the First Amendment, but I believe we must
use some common sense when interpreting it.*

PLANET EARTH/NATURE

◆ ◆ ◆

I believe nature is at its best during fall.

ANIMALS/PETS

◆ ◆ ◆

I believe cats like being aloof.

TEAMS

◆ ◆ ◆

I believe the 1964–65 Boston Celtics were the best basketball team ever. (Bill Russell was the league's MVP that year.)

ATHLETES

♦ ♦ ♦

I believe Michael Jordan can fly.

PEOPLE IN HISTORY

_____

_____

_____

_____

_____

_____

_____

_____

_____

_____

_____

_____

_____

_____

_____

_____

_____

_____

_____

◆ ◆ ◆

I believe Hitler was pure evil.

PEOPLE TODAY

_____

_____

_____

_____

_____

_____

_____

_____

_____

_____

_____

_____

_____

_____

_____

_____

_____

_____

◆ ◆ ◆

I believe Jesse Jackson is well-intentioned.

POLITICIANS

♦ ♦ ♦

*I believe our politicians will continue to disappoint us
until they change the campaign financing laws.*

ARTISTS

_____

_____

_____

_____

_____

_____

_____

_____

_____

_____

_____

_____

_____

_____

_____

◆ ◆ ◆

*I believe I would enjoy talking to any of the people
in any of Edward Hopper's paintings.*

WRITERS

♦ ♦.♦

I believe John Feinstein is the world's best golf writer.

BOOKS

_____

_____

_____

_____

_____

_____

_____

_____

_____

_____

_____

_____

_____

_____

_____

_____

_____

_____

_____

◆ ◆ ◆

I believe **The Stranger** *was Albert Camus's best book.*

TV Shows and Personalities

_____

_____

_____

_____

_____

_____

_____

_____

_____

_____

_____

_____

_____

_____

_____

_____

_____

_____

_____

◆ ◆ ◆

*I believe Jay Leno is the best right now, but
Johnny Carson is still the king of late-night TV.*

IDEAS

♦ ♦ ♦

I believe capital punishment is justified in cases
where a child has been killed or abused.

WORDS

♦ ♦ ♦

I believe **joy** *is one of the most descriptive words in the English language.*

THOUGHTS

_____

_____

_____

_____

_____

_____

_____

_____

_____

_____

_____

_____

_____

_____

_____

◆ ◆ ◆

I believe professional wrestling should be rated
for content and language just like the movies.

THE FUTURE

♦ ♦ ♦

I believe Colin Powell would be a very good president.

THE PAST

◆ ◆ ◆

*I believe the disco craze of the 1970s was a
cruel joke on my generation and was created and
perpetuated by the military-industrial complex.*

CITIES/COUNTRIES

◆ ◆ ◆

I believe Chicago will always be our second city.
(L.A. just doesn't have a heart.)

TRAVEL

_____

_____

_____

_____

_____

_____

_____

_____

_____

_____

_____

_____

_____

_____

_____

_____

◆ ◆ ◆

*I believe Midwest Express is the best airline
in North America.*

HOTELS/RESTAURANTS/RESORTS

◆ ◆ ◆

*I believe Aquavit is the best restaurant
in New York City.*

FOOD AND DRINK

_____

_____

_____

_____

_____

_____

_____

_____

_____

_____

_____

_____

_____

_____

_____

_____

_____

◆ ◆ ◆

I believe a martini should be very dry.

FASHION/CLOTHES

◆ ◆ ◆

I believe tank tops are a big fashion mistake for men!

ENTERTAINMENT

◆ ◆ ◆

I believe Big Bird understands his audience better
than any other entertainer.

HABITS

◆ ◆ ◆

I believe in being the first one to apologize
even if I wasn't the one in the wrong.

HABITS

◆ ◆ ◆

I believe in saying "please" and "thank you."

SELF-IMPROVEMENT

◆ ◆ ◆

I believe big things happen after you do the little things.

SELF-IMPROVEMENT

◆ ◆ ◆

I believe in using a dictionary
if I don't know how to spell a word.

DOCTORS/MEDICINE/HEALTH

◆ ◆ ◆

I believe doctors should at least look interested
when patients come to see them.

PROFESSIONS

◆ ◆ ◆

I believe there are two kinds of lawyers in the world—
constructive and destructive.

MUSINGS

❖ ❖ ❖

I believe the Force is within all of us.

MUSINGS

◆ ◆ ◆

*I believe McDonald's should introduce Happy Meals
for adults. (Adults like free stuff too.)*

SHOULD DO

_____

_____

_____

_____

_____

_____

_____

_____

_____

_____

_____

_____

_____

_____

_____

_____

_____

_____

◆ ◆ ◆

I believe I should start a diary.

HINTS/TIPS

♦ ♦ ♦

I believe a slow wallet can ruin a friendship.

PET PEEVES

❖ ❖ ❖

I believe what my grandmother taught me:
Walk on the right side of the sidewalk.

FULFILL YOUR DESTINY

◆ ◆ ◆

I believe that I will eventually find the perfect job.

POP CULTURE

◆ ◆ ◆

I believe Jerry Springer should be ashamed of himself.

TRADITIONS

_____
_____
_____
_____
_____
_____
_____
_____
_____
_____
_____
_____
_____
_____
_____
_____
_____
_____

◆ ◆ ◆

I believe in Santa Claus.

ATTRIBUTES

◆ ◆ ◆

I believe everyone has at least one talent
that he or she takes for granted.

ROMANCE

◆ ◆ ◆

*I believe kissing and making up is one of the
best things about marriage.*

RETAILERS/STORES

◆ ◆ ◆

I believe Target is the best mass-market merchandiser.

PRODUCTS

_____

_____

_____

_____

_____

_____

_____

_____

_____

_____

_____

_____

_____

_____

_____

_____

_____

◆ ◆ ◆

*I believe Bon Ami is the best household cleaner
on the market.*

INTROSPECTION

_____

_____

_____

_____

_____

_____

_____

_____

_____

_____

_____

_____

_____

_____

_____

_____

_____

_____

_____

◆ ◆ ◆

I believe my desire to "have it all" is unrealistic.

GOOD IDEAS

_____
_____
_____
_____
_____
_____
_____
_____
_____
_____
_____
_____
_____
_____
_____
_____
_____
_____
_____

◆ ◆ ◆

I believe in subscribing to my local newspaper.

EVERYDAY TIPS

◆ ◆ ◆

I believe good cookware does make life easier.

PLEASURES

_____

_____

_____

_____

_____

_____

_____

_____

_____

_____

_____

_____

_____

_____

◆ ◆ ◆

*I believe swing sets are enjoyed equally by
children and adults.*

THE WAY THINGS ARE

◆ ◆ ◆

I believe you are born either straight or gay.

DECISION TIME

◆ ◆ ◆

*I believe the drug war is a war we must fight to win
even if that means using the military.*

GOING OUT ON A LIMB

◆ ◆ ◆

I believe Elvis is dead.

DREAMS

◆ ◆ ◆

I believe in Martin Luther King Jr.'s dream.

CALL ME CONSERVATIVE

◆ ◆ ◆

I believe the least government is the best government.

CALL ME EDGY

◆ ◆ ◆

I believe coffee makes each day possible.

HOME/CAR/YARD

♦ ♦ ♦

I believe in checking the gas gauge before I drive off.

WHAT MATTERS TO YOU

◆ ◆ ◆

*I believe far too many questionable words are allowed
to air on TV and radio these days, especially
during prime time.*

AFFIRMATIONS

◆ ◆ ◆

I believe it's important to be enthusiastic at work and play.

SERIOUS SUBJECTS

◆ ◆ ◆

*I believe Jackie Robinson helped make America
a better place.*

ETHICAL CONSIDERATIONS

_____

_____

_____

_____

_____

_____

_____

_____

_____

_____

_____

_____

_____

_____

_____

_____

◆ ◆ ◆

*I believe stereotypes are right enough often enough
to be dangerous.*

THE OBVIOUS

◆ ◆ ◆

*I believe anybody who is cruel to animals
should be put in jail.*

BE REALISTIC

◆ ◆ ◆

I believe all adults should have up-to-date wills.

NOSTALGIA

_____

_____

_____

_____

_____

_____

_____

_____

_____

_____

_____

_____

_____

_____

_____

◆ ◆ ◆

I believe Lee Harvey Oswald was just a patsy.

SOCIAL ISSUES

_____

_____

_____

_____

_____

_____

_____

_____

_____

_____

_____

_____

_____

_____

_____

_____

◆ ◆ ◆

*I believe the United States is making progress in
race relations, but it will be another four or five
generations before race won't be much of an issue.*

SOCIAL ISSUES

—————————————————————————
—————————————————————————
—————————————————————————
—————————————————————————
—————————————————————————
—————————————————————————
—————————————————————————
—————————————————————————
—————————————————————————
—————————————————————————
—————————————————————————
—————————————————————————
—————————————————————————
—————————————————————————
—————————————————————————
—————————————————————————
—————————————————————————
—————————————————————————

◆ ◆ ◆

*I believe education should be everybody's top
social priority.*

REMINDERS

◆ ◆ ◆

I believe in stopping my car and helping turtles across the road.

REMINDERS

◆ ◆ ◆

I believe older people deserve my respect.

INVENTIONS

_____

_____

_____

_____

_____

_____

_____

_____

_____

_____

_____

_____

_____

_____

_____

_____

_____

_____

◆ ◆ ◆

I believe the remote control ranks as one of the
top ten inventions of all time.

TIME

◆ ◆ ◆

I believe I should have spent more time with
Mother before she died.

WARNINGS

◆ ◆ ◆

I believe in speaking to your audience, not over it.

ATTRIBUTES

_____

_____

_____

_____

_____

_____

_____

_____

_____

_____

_____

_____

_____

_____

_____

◆ ◆ ◆

I believe good character is more important than
tons of talent.

MORE MUSINGS

◆ ◆ ◆

I believe the egg came before the chicken.

MORE MUSINGS

◆ ◆ ◆

I believe shag carpeting disappeared for a reason.

SCIENCE

♦ ♦ ♦

*I believe space exploration is essential if mankind is
going to survive another thousand years on Earth.*

MANNERS/SOCIAL GRACE

◆ ◆ ◆

I believe in firm handshakes.

Do

◆ ◆ ◆

I believe I should read more.

FRIENDLY REMINDER

_____

_____

_____

_____

_____

_____

_____

_____

_____

_____

_____

_____

_____

_____

_____

_____

_____

_____

◆ ◆ ◆

I believe everybody loves to receive a compliment.

SECRET OF LIFE

_____

_____

_____

_____

_____

_____

_____

_____

_____

_____

_____

_____

_____

_____

_____

_____

_____

◆ ◆ ◆

_I believe the secret of life is having a
kind and generous heart._

SECRET OF LIFE

_____

_____

_____

_____

_____

_____

_____

_____

_____

_____

_____

_____

_____

_____

_____

◆ ◆ ◆

*I believe shorter is better when it comes to speeches,
presentations, and toasts.*

TRUISMS

◆ ◆ ◆

*I believe intelligence is ultimately measured
by accomplishment.*

IDENTITY

❖ ❖ ❖

I believe I am the same person I was twenty-five years ago; however, the mirror tells a different story.

CHOICES

♦ ♦ ♦

I believe Minute Maid orange juice tastes better than Tropicana.

JUST ACCEPT IT

❖ ❖ ❖

I believe birth order does influence our personalities.

CLICHÉS

◆ ◆ ◆

I believe life goes by way too fast.

CLICHÉS

◆ ◆ ◆

I believe practice makes perfect (or at least will help).

WISH LIST

◆ ◆ ◆

*I believe in world peace. (That is probably more
of a wish than a belief.)*

Wish List

_____

_____

_____

_____

_____

_____

_____

_____

_____

_____

_____

_____

_____

_____

_____

_____

_____

_____

◆ ◆ ◆

*I believe the world's leaders, including the pope,
need to deal with the issue of overpopulation.*

TAKING CARE OF BUSINESS

◆ ◆ ◆

I believe in knowing your competition.

TAKING CARE OF BUSINESS

_____

_____

_____

_____

_____

_____

_____

_____

_____

_____

_____

_____

_____

_____

_____

_____

_____

_____

◆ ◆ ◆

*I believe all successful people have made more
than their fair share of mistakes.*

GOALS AND STANDARDS

◆ ◆ ◆

I believe I will get a hole in one before I die.

ADMIRABLE TRAITS

♦ ♦ ♦

I believe in getting to work on time.

GIRL THING

◆ ◆ ◆

*I believe women—and women only—should decide
the abortion issue.*

BOY THING

_____

_____

_____

_____

_____

_____

_____

_____

_____

_____

_____

_____

_____

_____

_____

_____

◆ ◆ ◆

I believe **GoodFellas** *is the ultimate "guy" movie.*

KID THING

_____

_____

_____

_____

_____

_____

_____

_____

_____

_____

_____

_____

_____

_____

_____

◆ ◆ ◆

I believe little girls are sugar and spice
and all things nice.

ALL SO TRUE

◆ ◆ ◆

*I believe the Gettysburg Address is an
American treasure.*

REMEMBERING THE OBVIOUS

_____

_____

_____

_____

_____

_____

_____

_____

_____

_____

_____

_____

◆ ◆ ◆

I believe success begins with the following daily routine:
1. Wake up.
2. Get out of bed.
3. Shower.
4. Get dressed.
5. Go to work.

PRIORITIES

◆ ◆ ◆

I believe in taking lots of photographs and videos
of my family and friends.

GOD/CHURCH

◆ ◆ ◆

I believe God's greatest gift to mankind is free will.

PERSONAL RELIGION BELIEFS

_____

_____

_____

_____

_____

_____

_____

_____

_____

_____

_____

_____

_____

_____

_____

_____

_____

◆ ◆ ◆

*I believe Søren Kierkegaard is the
father of existentialism.*

PHILOSOPHICALLY SPEAKING

_____

_____

_____

_____

_____

_____

_____

_____

_____

_____

_____

_____

_____

_____

_____

_____

_____

_____

◆ ◆ ◆

*I believe America's ethnic differences will
eventually become one of its strengths.*

CONVICTIONS

_____

_____

_____

_____

_____

_____

_____

_____

_____

_____

_____

_____

_____

_____

_____

_____

_____

◆ ◆ ◆

I believe in signing organ donor cards.

QUALITIES

◆ ◆ ◆

*I believe heroes are normal people who know
their limitations but choose to challenge them.*

FUN TO THINK ABOUT

◆ ◆ ◆

I believe I exist.

QUOTES/REMARKS

_____

_____

_____

_____

_____

_____

_____

_____

_____

_____

_____

_____

_____

_____

_____

_____

◆ ◆ ◆

I believe Tennessee Williams was absolutely right
when he said: "The only thing worse than a liar
is a liar that's also a hypocrite!"

QUOTES/REMARKS

◆ ◆ ◆

I believe Robert Frost put life into
proper perspective when he wrote:
Forgive, O Lord, my little jokes on Thee
And I'll forgive Thy great big one on me.

BELIEFS ABOUT ME

_____

_____

_____

_____

_____

_____

_____

_____

_____

_____

_____

_____

_____

_____

_____

_____

_____

_____

◆ ◆ ◆

I believe I am the most normal person in my family.

BELIEFS ABOUT ME

◆ ◆ ◆

I believe in admitting my mistakes.

MONEY

◆ ◆ ◆

I believe in compound interest.

COMMON SENSE

❖ ❖ ❖

I believe you should turn off your cell phone in church, in restaurants, at lunch, at the movies, on the golf course, and at school plays and concerts.

ACTION

_____

_____

_____

_____

_____

_____

_____

_____

_____

_____

_____

_____

_____

_____

_____

_____

_____

_____

_____

◆ ◆ ◆

I believe you need to take your sense of humor
to work every day.

WISDOM

_____

_____

_____

_____

_____

_____

_____

_____

_____

_____

_____

_____

_____

_____

_____

_____

◆ ◆ ◆

I believe in hiring people who are smarter than I am.

HOW TO SUCCEED

♦ ♦ ♦

*I believe one hour of creative thinking is often
more productive than ten hours of analyzing minutiae.*

PURSUIT OF HAPPINESS

_____

_____

_____

_____

_____

_____

_____

_____

_____

_____

_____

_____

_____

_____

_____

◆ ◆ ◆

I believe in plastic surgery if it makes you feel better about yourself.

PEOPLE

_____
_____
_____
_____
_____
_____
_____
_____
_____
_____
_____
_____
_____
_____
_____
_____
_____

◆ ◆ ◆

*I believe Helen Keller was one of the most courageous
Americans in our history.*

MORE PEOPLE

♦ ♦ ♦

*I believe Yoko Ono is responsible for the breakup
of the Beatles.*

RESPONSIBILITIES

_____

_____

_____

_____

_____

_____

_____

_____

_____

_____

_____

_____

_____

_____

_____

_____

_____

◆ ◆ ◆

*I believe parents must accept the fact that they are
role models for their children.*

PEACE OF MIND

_____

_____

_____

_____

_____

_____

_____

_____

_____

_____

_____

_____

_____

_____

❖ ❖ ❖

*I believe the governments of the world should
set aside their differences and make a real effort to
save as many endangered animals as possible.*

CREATIVE THINKING

◆ ◆ ◆

*I believe thinking about the box is often more important
than thinking outside the box.*

ENVIRONMENT

♦ ♦ ♦

I believe in ZPG (zero population growth).

POSITIVE THINKING

◆ ◆ ◆

I believe in the American dream.

JUST DO IT

♦ ♦ ♦

I believe in acts of kindness.

WORRIES AND CONCERNS

◆ ◆ ◆

I believe Wal-Mart needs to landscape its parking lots.

BLESSINGS

◆ ◆ ◆

*I believe memories are treasures that are worth
far more than gold.*

KINDNESS

◆ ◆ ◆

I believe in saying "good morning" to my neighbors.

*Keep thinking and writing. The remaining pages
are for all of your other beliefs.*

I Believe

I Believe

I Believe

I Believe

I Believe

I Believe

I Believe

I Believe

I Believe

I Believe

I Believe

I Believe

I Believe